YELLOW

by Melanie Mitchell

first step nonfiction

Lerner Publications · Minneapolis

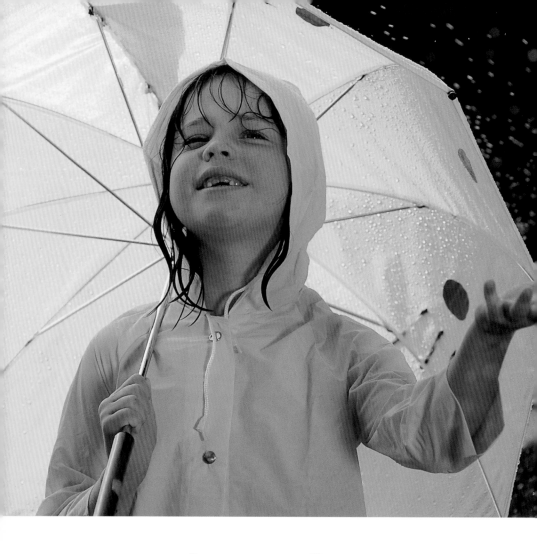

I see yellow.

The sun is yellow.

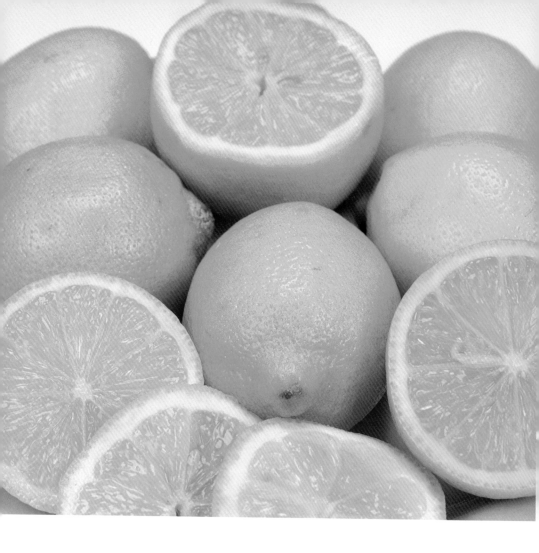

A lemon is yellow.

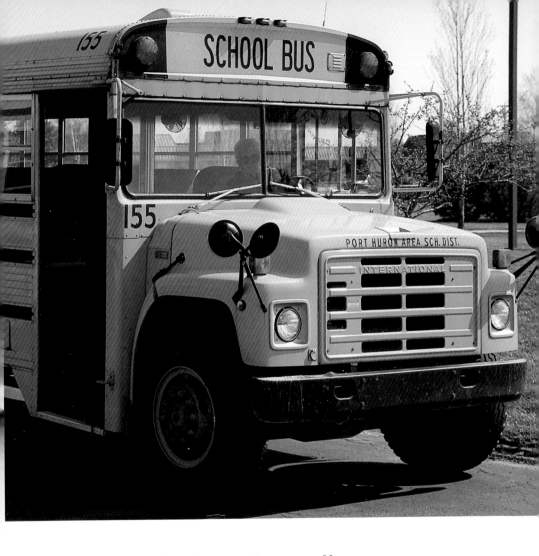

A bus is yellow.

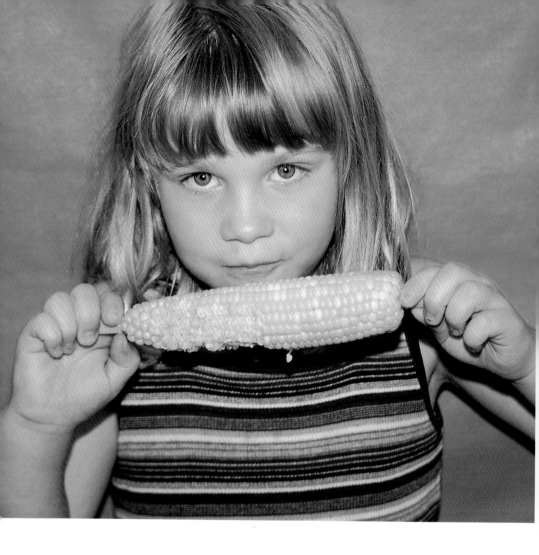

The corn is yellow.

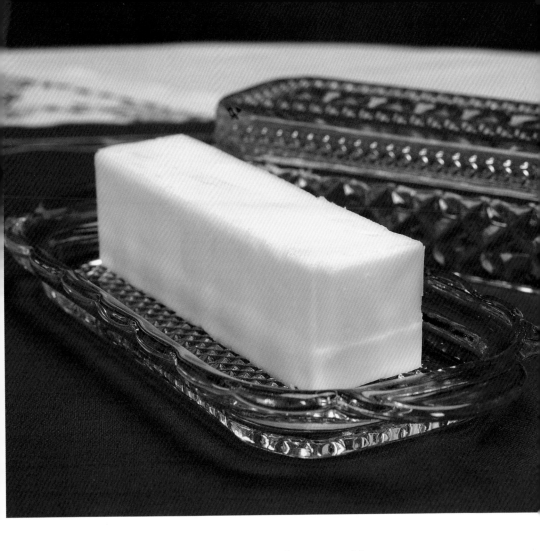

The butter is yellow.

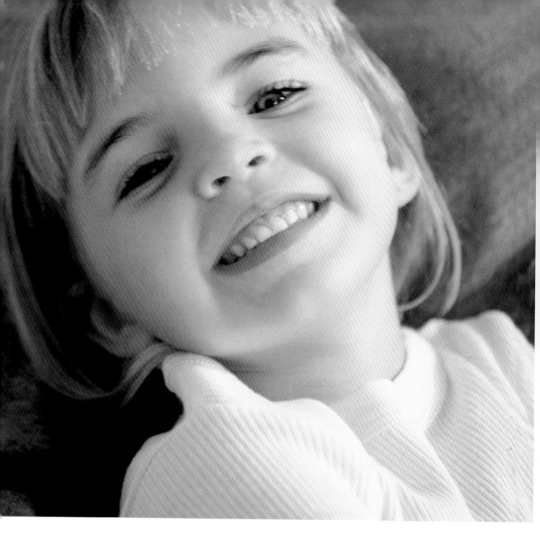

I like yellow!